CHILCOT

Richard Norton-Taylor
and Matt Woodhead

CHILCOT

OBERON BOOKS
LONDON

WWW.OBERONBOOKS.COM

First published in 2016 by Oberon Books Ltd
521 Caledonian Road, London N7 9RH
Tel: +44 (0) 20 7607 3637 / Fax: +44 (0) 20 7607 3629
e-mail: info@oberonbooks.com
www.oberonbooks.com

PB ISBN: 9781783197736
E ISBN: 9781783197743

Cover design by Joseph Priestley

Printed and bound by 4EDGE Ltd., Essex, United Kingdom.

Chilcot was commissioned by The Lowry & Battersea Arts Centre. It was developed and supported by The National Theatre Studio. The production had its world premiere at Lowry Studio on 26–28 May and Battersea Arts Centre on the 1–10 June 2016.

Introduction

The Chilcot inquiry into how and why Britain joined the US-led invasion of Iraq, widely seen as the most damaging foreign policy disaster in modern times, is an ideal candidate for a verbatim and documentary theatre production. Using the theatre as a platform in this way contributes to the democratic process.

The inquiry, set up by Gordon Brown in 2009, six years after the invasion, was crying out for a new audience. The devastating evidence it heard from senior ministers, military commanders, security and intelligence officers, civil servants and advisers, is in danger of being consigned to history.

Last year we quickly agreed that Chilcot urgently needed to be revisited. Richard had behind him the experience of the 'tribunal' verbatim plays performed at the Tricycle Theatre in Kilburn, northwest London, based on public inquiries and trials. The plays (all published by Oberon) include: *The Colour of Justice*, on the racist murder of the black teenager, Stephen Lawrence; *Bloody Sunday, Scenes from the Saville Inquiry* into the shooting of Irish civil rights marchers in Derry in January 1972; the *Nuremberg War Crimes Trial*; and *Justifying War*, based on the Hutton inquiry into the circumstances surrounding the death of the government's Iraqi weapons expert, David Kelly.

Matt and his verbatim company LUNG had recently successfully performed *The 56*, based on testimony from survivors of the Bradford City football stadium fire in 1985. Their second community based verbatim play *E15* examined the struggle by twenty-nine mothers to prevent families from being evicted and the housing crisis in Newham, east London. Both productions premiered at the Edinburgh Fringe Festival and toured nationally, platforming unheard voices across the country.

Many involved in the inquiry, especially Tony Blair, his former ministers and close advisers, insist there have been enough investigations into the circumstances leading up to the 2003 invasion of Iraq. It is time to move on, they insist. We profoundly disagree.

And other voices needed to be heard. We decided to give a platform to these voices through the play. They include: Iraq veterans; families of British soldiers killed during the conflict the invasion provoked; and also from Iraqis affected by the invasion. The interviews we conducted are interspersed with the Chilcot tribunal testimony.

One senior British military commander described the 2003 invasion as the 'original sin' which provoked years of violence, Sunni-Shia sectarian war, and from which the emergence of Isis sprung. Patrick Cockburn, the authoritative and respected British journalist writing about the Middle East, describes the 2003 invasion in his most recent book, *Chaos and Caliphate*, as the 'earthquake whose aftershocks we still feel'. He adds: 'It destroyed Iraq as a united country and nobody has been able to put it back together again.'

Nobody, apart from the dictator's henchmen, defended Saddam Hussein. The question was, why invade Iraq at a time extreme Islamist-based terrorism was by far the greatest threat to Britain and the west? Saddam was not linked to al-Qaeda. The question was posed when the head of MI5, Eliza (now Baroness) Manningham-Buller, gave evidence.

Asked by Chilcot whether, in her view, the invasion of Iraq substantially increased the terrorist threat to the UK, she replied, unequivocally, that yes, it did so. She added: 'We did not believe he (Saddam Hussein) had the capability to do anything much in the UK. That turned out to be the right judgment'.

Given his subsequent support for Muammar Gaddafi, the Libyan leader, Blair curiously told the Chilcot inquiry: 'As a matter of sensible foreign policy...the way to deal with one dictatorial threat is not to back another'.

At the time we were going to print (May 2016) Sir John Chilcot announced his inquiry's report will finally be published on 6 July. It consists of 2.6m words, about four times the length of Tolstoy's *War and Peace*. But there is a danger that this valuable evidence will be lost, smothered, and eclipsed by the consequences of the EU referendum vote on 23 June and by spin from all sides.

Britain is still suffering, directly or indirectly, from the invasion of Iraq. Sectarianism has divided Iraq and Isis has taken over significant areas of the country.

Chilcot offers audiences the opportunity to assess the key evidence for themselves, in some 20,000 words.

Richard Norton-Taylor and Matt Woodhead

About LUNG

Making theatre by communities, for communities and with communities, LUNG is a national touring theatre company, developing innovative and politically driven work that broadens horizons and investigates modern Britain.

Founded in Barnsley in 2016, LUNG frequently performs and develops new work with The Lowry, Battersea Arts Centre and The Civic in Barnsley. We are dedicated to producing new verbatim theatre as well as collaborating with new writers. Back home up north, LUNG also pursues an extensive education programme which specialises in bringing theatre into new communities across South Yorkshire.

2016, LUNG will be touring *The 56*, *E15* and *Dolly Wants to Die* across the UK.

Acknowledgements

With thanks to the National Theatre Studio, Battersea Arts Centre, The Lowry, Alex Ferris & Old Vic New Voices, The Guardian, NSDF, Military Families Against War, Veterans for Peace, Stop the War Coalition, Migrant Voice, Faith Forum, Iraqi Body Count, CAGE, Haifa Zangana, Diyan Zora, Hassan Abdulrazzak, Mark Townsend, Simon Hooper, Chris Thorpe, Helen Monks, Tamar Saphra, Simon Shepherd, Julia Ford, Nicholas Tennant, Jonathan Dryden-Taylor.

Special thanks to Rachel Twigg. Without your advice, help and support, none of this would have been possible.

We are also indebted to Asma (aka Smile Cookie) for her dedication and countless hours spent facilitating interviews across Jordan.

Chilcot was originally performed with six actors, multi-rolling all parts.

Original cast: Souad Faress, Thomas Wheatley, Jonathan Coote, Sanchia McCormack, Raad Rawi, Gary Pillai

Characters

The Chilcot Inquiry Panel

Sir John Chilcot
Baroness Una Prashar
Sir Roderic Lyne
Sir Lawrence Freedman
Sir Martin Gilbert

The Witnesses

Sir Mark Allen, Head of MI6 Counter Terrorism Operations
Sir Michael Wood, chief legal adviser at the Foreign
and Commonwealth Office
Lord Goldsmith, Attorney General

Hans Blix, chief UN weapons inspector in Iraq
Admiral Michael Boyce, chief of defence staff
Geoff Hoon, defence secretary
Jack Straw, foreign secretary
Tony Blair, prime minister
Alastair Campbell
Minister's director of communications and strategy
Clare Short, international development secretary
Unidentified MI6 witness
Eliza Manningham-Buller, head of MI5

The Interviewed
Oliver, A Civil Servant
Nick and Simon, UK veterans
Peter Brierley and Rose Gentle, military families
Shaikh Marwan Al Dulaimi,
Head of the Revolutionary Council
Ali, an Iraqi Civilian living in Basra
Nadia, an Iraqi Civilian living in Baghdad

Edited and compiled by Richard Norton-Taylor & Matt
Woodhead
Director: Matt Woodhead
Producer: Sarah Georgeson
Assistant Producer: Christabel Holmes
Lighting Designer: Will Monks
Set & Costume Designer: James Donnelly
Lighting and Video Designer: Will Monks
Sound Designer: Owen Crouch
Cover Art: Joseph Priestley

Setting

The action of the play is split between the evidence room at the
Chilcot Inquiry and in various one-on-one interview settings.

Authors' Note

All evidence has been taken directly from the evidence given
at the Chilcot Inquiry. None of the words of the witnesses who
gave evidence, or of the panel members who asked questions,
have been changed.

All interview material has been collected by Matt Woodhead &
Richard Norton-Taylor. Some names of those interviewed have
been changed to protect identities.

NADIA: On Thursday the bombing started. It was 4am. At that time my family was five sisters and one brother. We crawled into my mum and dad's bed and tried to sleep. George Bush said there was going to be a crusade and on Thursday it came to Baghdad.

I wanted to see what was going on so I ran downstairs and into the garden. I looked up at the sky and was just mesmerised by the image of the planes. My mother was shouting at me to come inside, but I couldn't move.

As the bombing got closer and more intense, I felt my world crumbling down. It was like seeing death in front of me and just waiting for it to come.

The siren sounded and I knew, yeah. That's war.

Private evidence of Witness Sir Mark Allen, Head of MI6 Counter Terrorism Operations, to the Chilcot Inquiry

Much of this evidence was redacted before publication

**** signify where a question / answer has been redacted or omitted by the inquiry on publication of the transcripts of this evidence session.

CHILCOT: Let's make a start. This session is being held in private because we recognise much of the evidence on the areas we want to cover will be sensitive, for example, on grounds of international relations or national security. What were your areas of responsibility in those different roles?

NARRATOR: This reply has been redacted.

ALLEN: ** * ** *****

CHILCOT: Thank you. One could go on, but I think I'll turn to Roderic Lyne at this point.

LYNE: On 30 November [2001] you had a meeting in Downing Street with Sir David Manning [Mr Blair's foreign policy adviser], at which you discussed a paper.

ALLEN: I do remember very clearly, about 4 o'clock in the afternoon, getting a telephone call from Number 10, 'David Manning wants to speak to you', and David coming on the line and saying, 'look, this Iraq stuff is building up apace. Can you just do me a quick paper, just bullet points, of key issues that we need to bear in mind to keep our balance and our perspective in considering Iraq as a rapidly expanding threat.'

So he wanted a sort of sedative paper, and he wanted it by 6 o'clock. So I had to cancel everything else I was doing and knock that up in about an hour.

It was sent off. The quickest communications between us and Number 10 would have been the Chief's driver. So yes, it would have gone through the Chief [of MI6, Sir Richard Dearlove].

LYNE: [The paper] begins: 'What can be done about Iraq? If the US heads for direct action, have we ideas which could divert them to an alternative course?'

LYNE: ****************************?

NARRATOR: Roderic Lyne's question has been redacted.

ALLEN: I think what I was trying to bring out was the hazards, the experience to date with Iraq, something about the nature of Iraq as a country. I wanted to arm David with background reminders that this is not going to be simple or straightforward. I don't think I had in my mind particular wheezes, schemes or policy programmes which could be followed up, simply to argue for caution and awareness of what a heavy matter Iraq could prove to be because it had been in the past.

LYNE: It is a list of hazards and warnings. It essentially reads – and your description of it that you have just given confirms this – as not a paper arguing for direct action, but warnings against.

NARRATOR: On 3 December [2001] three papers are sent by the Chief's office to Number 10.

The papers, since declassified, noted that 'the removal of Saddam remains a prize because it could give new security to oil supplies.' However, they warned that an attack on Iraq would mean: 'Increased distrust of US motives throughout the Islamic world. Confidence in HMG (the UK government), as a close US ally, also damaged'. They added: 'terrorists' motives and grievances reinforced... Anger and resentment in the Arab Street. The bombings will be seen as an attack on ordinary Arabs, rather than Saddam'.

The letters also warned: 'Accusations of double standards (one law for the Israelis; another for the Arabs).

ALLEN: I think it came out of the ground like a mist following the change of temperature on 9/11. I think it became clear to all of us that nothing short of decisive intervention in Iraq was going to satisfy the Americans.

LYNE: I would just like to look a little bit at the substance of paper. What did you see as the attractions of removing Saddam Hussein? What was the case that you were making here for regime change?

ALLEN: I remember saying to somebody at that time that the lack of our response to the re-emergence of Iraq as a serious regional power was like having tea with some very proper people in the drawing room and noticing that there was a python getting out of a box in one corner. I was very alarmed at the way that Iraq was eroding the sanctions regime and evading it.

The idea of putting an end to this problem was not something that I would advocate, but I could see the force of the desire to do it, to be decisive. The Foreign Office

3

position, well into 2002, was 'there's not going to be a war because there had been no second [UN]resolution, and the international community won't stand for it'.

LYNE: You touched on the kind of regime that might follow Saddam, and you said it would be important not to parachute a regime in from the external opposition. They would be regarded as US stooges. Then you said: 'The new government would need to be broadly based but predominantly Sunni.' How did you think that a change of regime could end up still with a predominantly Sunni regime in a country with a majority or largest ethnic grouping being Shi'ite? Having toppled the Sunnis, how were the Sunnis going to succeed the Sunnis?

ALLEN: There were a lot of Sunnis in Iraq who would have liked Iraq to be run differently. I don't think at this time it occurred to me that it was plausible to transfer an adversarial, party political, representational political system to Iraq. The idea that Iraqi Shias could be fitted out with Republican, Democrat, Lib Dem identities, organisations and run the difficult place which is Iraq, a place which has never had stable political geography.

GILBERT: One of the things you list, which seems to us important, you state that the government law officers are going to have to provide assurances of legality, and you say there has been a serious problem here. What problems had there already been with regard to legality of these concepts?

ALLEN: This was a considerable point of concern, not because we aimed to do something we knew was illegal, though of course, by definition, all MI6 activity was illegal, but because we didn't want to put our feet in the wrong place or get snagged.

LYNE: Do you think that MI6 got too close to the policy making, too involved in Number 10?

ALLEN: I think there's a high volume of urban myth to that effect abroad in the world, and many people are convinced of that. I think that we may not have been as wise as we would like to have been in retrospect, collectively. I don't think, in the circumstances of those days – completely different from my memory of top level consideration of intelligence in the Cold War – that we got too close to the sun. The Icarus metaphor is used time and again. It has limited applicability because Tony Blair was not the sun and [Sir Richard] Dearlove [the Chief of MI6] was not a child with wax wings. They were consenting adults, wrestling with unprecedented policy riddles.

PRASHAR: I want to cover issues to do with what we knew about Iraq.

ALLEN: About Iraq?

PRASHAR: Iraq, yes. What is your personal assessment of the government's pre-conflict knowledge of life in Iraq under Saddam on issues such as cultural and ethnic divisions?

ALLEN: Actually our knowledge of Iraq was very, very superficial. We were small animals in a dark wood with the wind getting up and changing direction the whole time. These were very, very difficult days. None of us had experience of our work being so critical to major policy dramas, and I venture in an ignorant kind of way to suggest you would have to go back to the Cuban missile crisis to find something similar.

The difficulty, I think, was the very early sense that we had that we were heading towards a war. That was not something that anybody welcomed.

Those of us who had been around ********************.

NARRATOR: This passage has been deleted.

ALLEN: We all knew perfectly well what a disaster for countless people a war was going to be. So there was no appetite. But there was a strong sense that that's the way we were heading.

Sir Michael Wood Legal Adviser for the Foreign and Commonwealth Office (26 January 2010)

CHILCOT: Good morning, ladies and gentlemen. Today, we are going to begin by hearing evidence on the legal issues surrounding the military action in Iraq. Our first witness this morning is Sir Michael Wood.

You were legal adviser at the Foreign and Commonwealth Office 2001 to 2006. I think it would be very helpful if you can just tell us whether you were ever asked to advise on the provisions of international law relevant to regime change in Iraq, who asked you, and what advice did you give?

WOOD: It was such an obvious point that kept on coming up; 'regime change is not a legal basis for the use of force'. It wasn't really controversial it went constantly into documents and was not, as far as I can recall, challenged by anyone.

The first possible basis [for the use of military force] would be self-defence, and it was clear to all the lawyers concerned that a factual basis for self-defence was not present, because there was not – Iraq was not engaged in an armed attack, nor was there an imminent armed attack on us or anybody else. So self-defence was ruled out.

The second possibility would have been the exceptional right to use force in the case of an overwhelming humanitarian catastrophe. This was the Kosovo argument, the argument we used in 1999. The third possible basis was with authorisation by the UN Security Council

PRASHAR: During this period, nobody challenged you, nobody disagreed with you?

WOOD: That's correct.

PRASHAR: This was the consistent view of you and your colleagues?

WOOD: Yes.

LYNE: Can we take your advice on the 24 January 2003 to the Private secretary to Mr Jack Straw? You say in this minute: 'I hope there is no doubt in anyone's mind that without a further decision of the UN Security Council, and extraordinary circumstances of which there is no sign, the United Kingdom cannot lawfully use force against Iraq. Can I ask why you felt it necessary to send this advice to the Foreign Secretary?

WOOD: It is something I didn't normally have to do, but I did it quite frequently during this period.

LYNE: How did he react to that advice?

WOOD: He took the view that I was being very dogmatic and that international law was pretty vague and that he wasn't used to people taking such a firm position.

LYNE: How would you describe the tone of that discussion?

WOOD: It was very amicable.

LYNE: Amicable?

WOOD: Yes.

LYNE: A friendly discussion, but a strong disagreement?

WOOD: Yes.

LYNE: Would you agree with the Foreign Secretary's characterisation in this minute of 29 January that 'international law is an uncertain field'?

WOOD: It is rather a general statement. Where I would strongly disagree is where he says: 'because there is no court to decide these matters'. He is somehow implying that one can therefore be more flexible and that, I think, is probably the opposite of the case. I think, because there is no court, those taking decisions have to be all the more scrupulous in adhering to the law.

FREEDMAN: Just to be clear what's going on, whatever disagreements you may have had with Jack Straw, in the end, a decision was for the Attorney General.

WOOD: The Attorney should, in my view, have been asked at an earlier stage and given rolling advice as the situation developed.

PRASHAR: So you think the Attorney wasn't involved in a timely way? Is that what you were suggesting?

WOOD: I think his formal advice came very late.

Evidence of Witness Lord Goldsmith, Attorney General, to the Chilcot Inquiry (27 January 2010)

CHILCOT: Good morning ladies and gentlemen. We welcome Lord Goldsmith who was Attorney General for England, Wales and Northern Ireland until June 2007. Good morning, Lord Goldsmith.

GOLDSMITH: Good morning.

PRASHAR: Were you aware of discussions across Whitehall during the first half of 2002 on the possible basis of use of force?

GOLDSMITH: Not really. It was obvious to me from the press that this was where we were coming to, and, therefore, I wanted to understand --

PRASHAR: So you were surmising all this from the press?

GOLDSMITH: I could see from the press what was being said by President Bush.

PRASHAR: So what you are saying is that, during the first half of 2002, you were not asked to provide advice on a legal basis for military action?

GOLDSMITH: No.

PRASHAR: I think you wrote to Geoff Hoon [Defence Secretary] on 28 March [2002]?

GOLDSMITH: Yes.

PRASHAR: Can you tell me what you were concerned about?

GOLDSMITH: He had, in an interview with Jonathan Dimbleby, expressed himself with apparent clarity and repeatedly – it wasn't just a single remark, saying that there was a clear basis for military action at that stage, without any further authority. I think he was wrong in any event. And so I wrote to him to make clear that I was unhappy about that

PRASHAR: Can you recall what his response was?

GOLDSMITH: His response was – he said that, if I'm allowed to refer to this. It has been – I know there is a bit of an issue, which is frustrating, about what has and has not been declassified.

CHILCOT: Can I just say, since you say that, the frustration is shared.

GOLDSMITH: I achieved my purpose of making it clear I didn't want to see senior ministers making apparently authoritative statements on behalf of HM Government about the use of force before I had even been asked to express any view about it.

PRASHAR: Now, can we come to the meeting that you attended on 23 July [2002] at Downing Street, when I think you said you expressed the view that self-defence and humanitarian intervention would provide no basis for use of force?

GOLDSMITH: From what I then knew. I expressed my view.

PRASHAR: You followed this up with the written advice?

GOLDSMITH: I followed this up with a written advice.

PRASHAR: Were you asked to do that or did you do it of your own volition?

GOLDSMITH: I did it of my own volition because I knew that the Prime Minister was going to see President Bush in the United States. I knew that one of the topics of conversation at least was going to be the Iraq issue. I wasn't asked for it. I don't, frankly, think it was terribly welcome.

PRASHAR: Were you encouraged to put your advice in writing?

GOLDSMITH: No, I wasn't.

PRASHAR: Sir Michael Wood [The Foreign Office's chief legal adviser] wrote to [The Foreign Secretary] Jack Straw, and Jack Straw replied: 'I take note of your advice, but I do not accept it.'

GOLDSMITH: Yes.

PRASHAR: You responded to this note expressing your view about the role of the legal officers. Do you want to expand on that?

GOLDSMITH: Yes, I'm grateful, thank you. I was unhappy when I saw that. I had always taken the view in government that they should express their views, however unwelcome they might be.

PRASHAR: Is it normally called 'speaking truth unto power'?

GOLDSMITH: Certainly. I have always taken the view – and I speak to officers in the legal services frequently– and I would say, 'Your job is to tell ministers what they need to hear, not what they would like to hear'.

PRASHAR: On 7 November [2002], you met the Foreign Secretary. Was the purpose of the meeting to make clear to him that he should not take it for granted that it would be 'all right on the night?'

GOLDSMITH: Probably that's right.

PRASHAR: What did you mean by it would not be 'all right on the night'?

GOLDSMITH: So far as United Nations authority was concerned, there needed at least to be a further United Nations Security Council Resolution.

LYNE: It is very important whether there had to be a further decision by the [UN] Security Council.

GOLDSMITH: Yes. That is the point about which argument has raged. My advice remained preliminary until February [2003]. It remained preliminary until February, because I was still conducting my enquiries and researches.

On, I think, 27 February, I met in Downing Street with, again, the Prime Minister's advisers and I told them then that, following my visit to the United States, I was of the view there was a reasonable case that a second UN Resolution was not necessary and that was sufficient to constitute a green light.

PRASHAR: Am I right in confirming that it was your provisional view until February that a second [UN] resolution was actually necessary?

GOLDSMITH: Yes.

LYNE: Thank you. You went to Washington on 10 February 2003.

GOLDSMITH: I talked to a number of people. They were absolutely speaking with one voice. They were very clear that what mattered to President Bush was 'the one thing that mustn't happen is that by going down this UN route, we then find we lose the freedom of action we think we now have'.

LYNE: If I can fly you back –

GOLDSMITH: Please, fly me back!

LYNE: If I can fly you back to London, you get back here, I think, on 11 February.

For the first time at this stage you stated that you were prepared to accept that a reasonable case could be made that the existing UN Security Council resolution 1441 revived the authorisation to use force?

GOLDSMITH: You make a judgment. I wanted to sort of underline to the Prime Minister that I was saying that reasonable case is enough. So that is the green light. But I want to underline, 'Please don't misunderstand, a reasonable case doesn't mean of itself that, if this matter we're to go to court, you would necessarily win'.

GILBERT: At that time, were you aware of [the Foreign Office chief legal adviser] Sir Michael Wood's advice to the Foreign Secretary that to advocate the use of force without, as he put it, a credible legal base, would be to advocate the commission of a crime of aggression and would expose members of the armed forces to charges of murder?

GOLDSMITH: I don't know whether I was aware of his view particularly.

GILBERT: The adoption of the statute of the International Criminal Court, was that an added factor with regard to potential legal action?

GOLDSMITH: It was an important issue. I now recognise that it wasn't good enough to say, 'There is a reasonable case' and I reached the view that, on balance, the better view was that it was lawful and that's why I came out with that.

LYNE: The prime minister's personal future was at stake, the government's future perhaps was at stake, [there] was huge pressure on the government at this point and you must have been conscious of that. Did it weigh on you?

GOLDSMITH: No.

LYNE: Did the international consequences of telling the Grand Old Duke of York, the chief of defence staff in this case, that he had to take his troops down from the top of the hill, not also weigh upon you?

GOLDSMITH: No.

LYNE: Then you saw the Foreign Secretary. What was the main thrust of your discussion with him?

GOLDSMITH: 'There is a risk that we will be taken to court if the decision is taken to go'.

PRASHAR: You would say there was never a full discussion in Cabinet about your opinion which was caveated and was finely balanced?

GOLDSMITH: The Cabinet, I'm sure, knew that there were two points of view because they had been well-travelled in the press.

This an issue of intense debate, politically and academically. Whether or not the military intervention was right or wrong, I don't think is for me to judge, but so far as the legality is concerned, I did reach the view then, and still am of the opinion, that it was lawful.

OLIVER: I'm an Arabic speaker. Because of my experience in the region, I was approached and asked in October 2002 whether I would be willing to get involved in planning for the possibility of military action in Iraq. Things seemed extremely odd. Once I became a part of the Iraqi Planning Unit, there was this assumption that – although it wasn't explicitly stated – war was going to happen. Straight away it felt like we were jumping down the wrong rabbit holes, focusing on how to print currency without Saddam's face on it – which suggested regime change was the real aim of the game – rather than rebuilding Iraq after the war.

Was there any discussion about the legality of the war in the planning meetings? Not that I recall. It was just assumed. A couple of weeks before the invasion I was briefed about a meeting at 10 Downing Street involving the Chief of the Defence Staff, the Foreign Secretary and the Defence Secretary. When Tony Blair asked the question 'what happens if we don't go?' he was told that it would set back our relations with America by 15 to 17 years. At that point one got the feeling that the decision wasn't based on legality but on our relationship with the US.

I was also ordered to give the dodgy dossier to a head of state in another country whose support we wanted. I remember sitting up in bed, reading it thinking it was an unutterable pile of dribble. It was all supposititious, allegations, weasely worded and not backed with any hard evidence or intelligence. I was astonished that this was the justification for a decision on going to war. I duly handed the dossier over and he asked for my thoughts. All I could say was it was sufficient enough to have convinced Tony Blair, ministers and the British government. He said 'well in that case it is good enough for me'.

There was a febrile atmosphere. The momentum was unstoppable. You got a feeling we'd put everything in place and why bother going to the expense if we weren't going to do it? It's a bit like the emperor's new clothes. When you've got late night meetings, phone calls, Number 10, the White House; the wagons get drawn in a circle and perspective is lost. Ministerial approval the military side wasn't anything anybody was taking seriously. When I asked whether decisions in the UK Area of Operations had been approved by Ministers, I was told 'well, that's what the American's want us to do'. Military planning was just rubber stamped. I mean as far as post invasion reconstruction was concerned, I was in Permanent Joint Headquarters in Northwood when the revised planning schedule came off the fax machine. This was just a couple weeks before the invasion.

I have spent my life in service of Queen and Country. My career has been to represent a system that is supposed to set an example to be followed by the rest of the world. But how many dead? How many continue to die because of what we did in Iraq? Each one was a mother, father, cousin, neighbour – and I played a role in that. It seems to be a universal British, American, Russian policy to support insurgency in the Middle East and it getting out of control. We did it in Afghanistan, it's happening now in Libya and Syria. In Iraq we lit the fuse. We couldn't control what happened next.

Evidence of Witness Admiral Lord Boyce to the Chilcot Inquiry (3 December 2009)

CHILCOT: I wonder if we could invite you, Lord Boyce, to explain your role.

BOYCE: I was chief of the defence staff.

LYNE: At what point in this period after 9/11 did the Ministry of Defence start thinking about the contingency – it was no more than that – of full-scale military action against Iraq and discussing it informally with your counterparts in the United States?

BOYCE: In the latter part of 2001, we had also heard the rumour that there was talk in the United States about effort to try to tie in Iraq with those who had been involved in Al-Qaeda in the 9/11 bombings.

We absolutely did not want to get involved in such conversations. Hardly surprising, because from about October onwards, we were heavily involved in the war in Afghanistan,

LYNE: If we carry that forward into the first four months of 2002, and particularly after President Bush's Axis of Evil speech, was this cloud beginning to appear on the horizon? Were you beginning to have to think about it a bit more then?

BOYCE: Yes,

LYNE: Could you both perhaps tell us how the MoD contributed to the Prime Minister's briefing [before] his important meeting with President Bush at [his Texas ranch at] Crawford [in April 2002]

BOYCE: Certainly, the process which we believed to be absolutely fundamental was that things should be done through the United Nations and not some sort of separate coalition effort.

FREEDMAN: On the question of force generation did you get a sense from the Americans, even, say, by May [2002], as to when they were thinking an operation might take place? Because presumably, given the long lead times you have talked about, we would have needed to start getting things moving.

BOYCE: But it is important to realise that I was not allowed to speak, for example, to the Chief of Defence Logistics – I was prevented from doing that by the Secretary of State for Defence [Geoff Hoon], because of the concern about it becoming public knowledge that we were planning for a military contribution which might have derailed the activity going on in the United Nations.

Why is that important? Because if you are doing an armed operation, you are going to have to take up ships from trade to get your forces out there, you're going to have a huge amount of logistic planning and to start buying in equipment, which the armed forces didn't have because they weren't funded to have ourselves the right level of preparation. Drawing money out of the Treasury is like getting blood out of a stone anyway. That just provided another impediment to fast process.

LYNE: By and large, if we were going in, you were in favour of going in with a larger package?

BOYCE: If they had chosen to go on their own, they [the US] could have done so. They had the capability and the numbers to do so, but I think they very much wanted to have us there as an ally, as another flag.

FREEDMAN: Multiple flags basically means we are there to provide political solidarity.

BOYCE: Absolutely. The other point on influence and aftermath, I could not get across to them the fact that the coalition would not be seen as a liberation force where flowers would be stuck at the end of rifles and that they would be welcomed and it would all be lovely.

When I said, 'This is not going to happen. There may be six hours of euphoria, but not much after that' and I think, as far as the Pentagon was concerned, they just thought that Iraq would be fine on the day, that, having knocked Saddam Hussein down, the place suddenly would be a lovely democracy and everybody would be happy.

LYNE: What were the consequences for us of having to act in this rush? Were our own commanders entirely clear on their role, on what they were being asked to do? Had there been time for our forces to train properly? Had there been time for them to acclimatise? Were they fully equipped?

BOYCE: It left us with some very short timelines, but I am confident they were properly equipped.

LYNE: Right down to the sort of details I mentioned —

BOYCE: Yes.

LYNE: — like body armour, boots and so on?

BOYCE: — I'm not familiar with the detail of things such as body armour. The unfortunate thing about going to war is that some people are going to get killed.

CHILCOT: Turning to the legal issue, you asked for, and got, a certificate from the Attorney General that it was lawful to go forward. It is in the nature of legal opinions that is they tend to be complex, they tend to be caveated, there tend to be arguments, but you needed a black and white certificate, you asked for it, and you got it. That was it?

BOYCE: Yes, it was something which I had told the Prime Minister that I would need at the end of the day, particularly for, my constituency, in other words, my soldiers, sailors and airmen and their families had to be told that what they were doing was legal.

LYNE: You said at the outset that all the way through, our policy was geared to going through the United Nations and it was geared, of course, to the disarmament of Iraq, and that was right up to March of 2003. But in the end, we were in a situation in which we went into this conflict without the approval of a second United Nations Security Council Resolution.

BOYCE: I always made it perfectly clear to the Prime Minister face-to-face, that if we were invited to go into Iraq, we had to have a good legal basis for doing so, which obviously a second resolution from the UN would have completely nailed. I was absolutely prepared to unhook ourselves.

LYNE: So you could have had your forces deployed out there but you would have said, 'They are not going to cross the start line'.

BOYCE: Absolutely.

LYNE: Would that not have been humiliating?

BOYCE: We are a democracy. If Parliament said we were not to engage, we would not engage.

LYNE: What would it have done for our relations with the United States, including our very important military relationship?

BOYCE: The [Americans] understood absolutely that if Parliament had said no, we would not be going.

LYNE: Were you clear in your own mind what the Prime Minister's objectives were?

BOYCE: To try to persuade Saddam Hussein to give up his weapons of mass destruction.

LYNE: But the American policy was explicitly and overtly to change the regime in Iraq?

BOYCE: Yes, it was and our policy absolutely specifically was not that, not regime change.

LYNE: The wider risks. You identified this risk when you briefed the Prime Minister on 15 January [2003] 'Aftermath planning was still quite immature and any rapid regime collapse followed by a power vacuum could result in internecine fighting between the Shia and Sunni populations, particularly in Baghdad, and adventuring by adjacent countries and ethnic groups that irretrievably fractured the country.' So you had got it pretty well right.

CHILCOT: A senior American general – I am afraid his name has gone from my head – who before the invasion expressed the view that very large number of troops would be required?

BOYCE: Shineski.

CHILCOT: So there were divided opinions even in the American military about the aftermath –

BOYCE: Not divided for very long, because he got fired.

CHILCOT: Just looking back across Whitehall and your position as the head of the armed services, do you think that the overall coordination of the UK effort, UK PLC, in 2002/3 as it applied to Iraq was an effective coordination effort or not?

BOYCE: No, not really. What we lacked was any sense of being at war. I suspect if I asked half the Cabinet were we at war, they wouldn't know what we were talking about. So there was a lack of political cohesion at the very top. In Iraq's case, possibly because some people were not happy about what we were doing anyway.

FREEDMAN: Do you imagine a point in terms of the questions that had been posed to you by Mr Blair is there a war winning strategy, you would have had to say 'No, there isn't'?

BOYCE: You can always have everything you want from the Prime Minister, but the fact is the Treasury is inherently unable to deliver money unless it is actually beaten over the head.

There is no point being told 'Here is an Urgent Operational Requirement for a nice gizmo, a nice new piece of kit which you can only have, by the way, in theatre', if the person operating that kit doesn't see it for the first time until he actually gets to theatre, because he will die trying to learn how to use it. If you were really on a proper war footing that wouldn't happen I don't think. I don't think the Treasury ever thought we were on a war footing. We were.

Evidence of Witness Hans Blix to the Chilcot Inquiry (27 July 2010).

CHILCOT: Welcome to our witness Dr Hans Blix. You served as the Chairman for the United Nations Monitoring, Verification and Inspection Commission, which I think we are allowed to call UNMOVIC, until the end of June 2003. What I want to ask you about is the various assessments on Iraq's weapons of mass destruction.

BLIX: It seemed plausible to me at the time, and I also felt, like most people at the time, that Iraq retained weapons of mass destruction. I did not say so publicly. I said it perhaps to Mr Blair in September 2002 privately.

FREEDMAN: Just then to confirm what you have just told us, your feeling at the time was that there probably was something there?

BLIX: Yes.

FREEDMAN: And that, as you say, you were sharing quite a broad consensus. I would just be interested in your views at this point about the difficulty of modulating assessments of this sort.

BLIX: On the nuclear side we were fairly sure in 1998 there was hardly anything left. We wanted to close the [file] but in the autumn of 2002 we began to hear about the contract allegedly made with Niger about the import of raw uranium.

The Niger document was scandalous. The International Atomic Energy Agency could have concluded a day that this document – which had been dancing between the Italians and the British and the Americans and the French – was a forgery.

LYNE: In terms of your broad judgments about cooperation [UN] resolution 1441 [in November 2002] had demanded immediate, unconditional and active cooperation [from Saddam Hussein to comply with disarmament obligations] Had Iraqi behaviour at any point corresponded to that?

BLIX: They had not been immediate, no.

LYNE: Even under what was obviously growing threat of military action, after three and a half months they had not opened the doors widely enough to convince you that they really had nothing to hide?

BLIX: I had said on some occasions it is not enough to open doors. You also have to be proactive. I think they were coming to be proactive, but it was rather late.

LYNE: Now if you felt that the Americans had misinterpreted Iraqi behaviour and that Iraq was genuinely cooperating, could you not have said very starkly to the Security Council that you really believed that Iraq was now cooperating in a way that did not make action appropriate?

BLIX: I would have felt a little presumptuous telling the Council exactly what to do. The decisive time for responsibility for going to the war is what the US and UK knew in March 2003. If the US had kept the pressure 100,000 men or whatever it was and sounded threatening, maybe we would have had the same cooperation, but once they went up to 250,000 men, and the time March was approaching, I think it was almost unstoppable.

After March the heat would go up in Iraq and it would be difficult to carry out warfare. The whole military timetable was not in sync with the diplomatic timetable. The diplomatic timetable would have allowed more inspections. UK wanted more inspections, but the military timetable did not permit that. As I have said, sometimes perhaps a little roughly, the UK remained a prisoner on that train. I made the remark that I cited many times, that: wouldn't it be paradoxical for you to invade Iraq with 250,000 men and find very little?

CHILCOT: I should like to ask you, Dr Blix if you have further reflections on lessons out of the Iraq experience.

BLIX: I am delighted that I think your intention is to draw lessons from the Iraq war rather than anything else, and I think that 'when can states go to war' still remains a vitally important issue.

SIMON: I was sixteen when I joined the army. My dad had to sign the papers to allow me to join. He wasn't too keen but I whinged until I got what I wanted. By the time the 2003 invasion came around I couldn't wait to get involved in an actual war. I mean, that's what we'd trained for.

NICK: Grandad was the hero of my family. We grew up badgering him to show us his medals. They were in a battered old envelope stuffed away in what we called the shit draw, which is where we kept lighters and bits of string. My imagination was always captured by Remembrance Sunday at the Cenotaph, watching those old soldiers marching down with their medals. I was thirteen when I joined the army cadets. That's when I fell in love with soldiering.

SIMON: You could tell the invasion was rushed because there was a lack of equipment and nobody had a clue what was happening. We were sat in Kuwait for about five or six weeks. I mean we got most of the news we needed off the BBC.

NICK: After SAS selection, I was deployed to Baghdad with thirty other guys. Our mission was to detain high value targets involved in the insurgency.

You'd fly out in helicopters at night. There's a curfew going on, so the streets were empty. With shotguns, assault rifles, grenades, crowbars, cuffs you'd sneak up and put explosives on someone's house. You'd blow the front doors and go through every room, dragging people out. Women and children in one room – you'd hold them at gun-point – while any male over sixteen had a hood on their head, their hands tied and was coming with us. Within twenty minutes your dad, your husband, your brother is gone.

Back at our base, we would leave them against the back wall, sort of spread eagled. Then the interrogation team would take over in a porta cabin in an American compound. SAS could detain, but not arrest anyone. An Arresting American officer did that so no one was ever in British custody. It was a legal loophole.

It was no big secret these people were being tortured in American detention centres. We heard first hand these men were being held in rows of dog kennels out in the sun. Interrogators used cattle prods, water boarding, threats of assassination – that kind of stuff. Only 5% of the people we carried out these attacks on were found to be involved in the insurgency.

It was all part of this process within the military of compartmentalisation. If you want to carry out a heinous crime, you split that crime up into small parts that are easy to do. Everyone plays their little part.

SIMON: In terms of combatting roadside bombs, the British army had electronic counter measures. This would block the signal coming from any enemy device – mobile phones, remote control cars – trying to detonate bombs. The Americans, however, had a system called Warlock which transmitted on every frequency in the known universe. The idea was to detonate roadside bombs well away from American soldiers. Explosions happened randomly. Nine times out of ten, civilians were killed.

It was on my second tour of Iraq. I was on foot patrol around the main British base and it was something that caught your eye; somebody wearing a Newcastle shirt in Iraq. We got talking and it turned out the British were detaining his brother in a makeshift detention centre inside the camp. But he was just a normal lad who you'd meet down the pub. It was a moment of clarity for me. I just thought I've got more in common with this bloke than half the idiots sitting behind the fence.

By the 22 April I made the decision. I got back to the UK and I thought that's me, I'm out.

NICK: When I got back from Iraq, every day I was just thinking what the fuck am I doing out there? What am I involved in? And every day I would come to the same conclusion – I can't carry on.

SIMON: Iraq is just a part of my past that I want to forget.

NICK: I was a part of this gang that were the main instigators of the chaos that is consuming the Middle East. It was only in prisons the resistance got organised. It was there they stated to form units and make plans for when they got out. We detained 25,000 men and out of twenty-five ISIS commanders, seventeen or eighteen have been through internment in Iraq.

SIMON: The British army are the architects of all the death and destruction you see across the Middle East on TV every night. I am deeply ashamed when I see pictures of small children washed up on Greek beaches. I live with that every day.

NICK: They talk about the fallen dead, but no one falls. Soldiers are blown to pieces, civilians are dragged from their homes at night. Soldiers don't sacrifice themselves. They are sacrificed.

You're blind to certain things as a kid. Looking back, my grandad only let me see his medals twice or three times. He served thirty-five years in the navy but he never went to a remembrance parade. I can't even remember him wearing a poppy.

Don't thank me for my service.

SIMON: Don't thank me for my service.

CHILCOT: Good afternoon everyone and welcome to our witness the Rt. Hon Jack Straw MP. You were Foreign Secretary from mid-2001 to mid-2006. I'll ask Sir Roderic Lyne to open the questions.

LYNE: If we get to the situation as the Prime Minister was approaching his meeting at Crawford with the President in April 2002. This was a critical time before we get set on a particular course. At that stage the Cabinet Office produces an option paper. Can you tell us to what extent there was a real debate about different strategic options?

STRAW: Let me be clear about this: that whatever the policy of the United States, which, as it happens was for regime change was off the agenda and also self-evidently unlawful.

LYNE: Was that also the Prime Minister's view?

STRAW: The Prime Minister was as well aware as I was. That military action for regime change, could not be an objective of British foreign policy. If I may, I think the best way to find that out is to ask him.

LYNE: But you say that you were having a debate with him about it.

STRAW: Look, we are two different people.

LYNE: But in one government?

STRAW: Of course, and we came to --

LYNE: I'm trying to work out what the government's policy was.

FREEDMAN: On 15 February (2003), there is the most enormous demonstration in the UK and elsewhere against the war. Was there a point, when you, colleagues, felt, 'This isn't going where we wanted it to go. Let's stop and think, and question, do we need to take another course?'

STRAW: Certainly I was profoundly concerned about the anger of a very large proportion of the British public, which included many personal friends. My constituency of Blackburn has a very large population of people of Asian heritage and Muslim faith, and most of those were very angry.

FREEDMAN: Was there any point at which you thought you could not go along with this?

STRAW: I never got to that point. Did I ever think I'm going to resign over this? No, I didn't. I mean, we all have our bottom lines. Did I understand the nature of the responsibilities on me? Yes, I did, for sure, and weighed them very heavily.

FREEDMAN: Thank you very much.

PRASHAR: I want to look at the question of the relationship with the Foreign Office legal advisers told us why did your public statements and conversations not reflect the advice that you had been given?

STRAW: I was actually very, very, careful in studying and acknowledging the legal advice. I never ignore advice. I gave it the most careful attention.

PRASHAR: We are not suggesting you ignored it, because you said you read it, you noted it, but you did not accept it

STRAW: Sorry and the legal advice he offered, frankly, was contradictory, and I think I was entitled to raise that.

CHILCOT: You think that, with hindsight, at any rate, when the issue is as big at this that it was right to call the Attorney General [about the legality of going to war with Iraq] when the policy was settled?

STRAW: The short answer to your question, Sir John, is yes we all have to learn lessons from this.

CHILCOT: You have said the Cabinet needed to know where it stood in legal terms in order to address the key moral as well as political issues. Could it actually do that without being fully alive to the fact that the legal arguments were finely balanced?

STRAW: I just want to say this about legal advice at that stage: what was required – at that stage, was essentially a yes/no decision from the Attorney General, The Cabinet was composed of some very strong-minded people: John Prescott, Gordon Brown, David Blunkett, None of these were wilting violets, What they wanted to know was what the answer was.

GILBERT: I'd like to look back five days before 17 March [2003]. In *A Journey* Mr Blair recalls you warning him about the perils of taking military action in Iraq without a second UN resolution and we have also heard from a witness whom we have agreed not to identify who said: 'I recall a meeting with the Prime Minister and the Foreign Secretary said: "If you want to avoid your own resignation, Prime Minister, you still have an opportunity and here it is. You have a way out and why don't you take it?"' Was your position at that meeting one of advocating to Mr Blair that he should not commit British troops to military action?

STRAW: I was – I mean – I don't think anybody was keen on military action, and it's horrible and people are going to get killed. I also felt that as I owed the Prime Minister my loyalty, I also owed him the best and most robust advice I could give him and that was always my approach in dealing with Prime Ministers.

CHILCOT: Thank you. Can I then in that case, Mr Straw, invite your own reflections on this whole Iraq experience?

STRAW: The first thing I wanted to do was to express again my deep sorrow and regret for the loss of life and the injuries of our forces, coalition forces, many civilians of Iraqi and every other nationality who lost their lives in this conflict. I hope I am able to say that I do believe that the action we took was justified. As I was putting it together thoughts of what I wanted to say in conclusion today, I was reminded of a very telling phrase in E H Carr's book about what is history in which he says: 'Events which are now long in the past were once in the future.'

Looking at Iraq, there is a sort of conventional wisdom that everything that did happen was pre-planned, was inevitable and occurred to a sinister design of President Bush and Prime Minister Blair. That was not the case at all, least of all for Prime Minister Blair.

Evidence of Witness Geoff Hoon, Defence Secretary, to the Chilcot Inquiry (19 January 2010)

CHILCOT: We would like to welcome Geoff Hoon, Defence Secretary until May 2005.

LYNE: To what extent were you, as Defence Secretary, privy to the Prime Minister's exchanges with President Bush orally and in writing, in the course of 2002 about Iraq?

HOON: An almost impossible question to answer. My impression from Alastair is that there were probably other rather more private communications that may have taken place. The Prime Minister was a great note writer and it would not surprise me at all that there were private notes that he would send to the President that I would not necessarily have been privy to.

LYNE: If he was writing notes that could be read by the recipient as committing Britain to military action, wouldn't you have expected, as Defence Secretary, to have been consulted?

HOON: I would have been, and that is why I don't believe he was ever unconditionally committing us to anything.

LYNE: Alastair Campbell described the tenor of this correspondence as: 'We share the analysis, we share the concern, we are absolutely with you in making sure that Saddam Hussein is faced up to his obligations and that Iraq is disarmed. If that can't be done diplomatically and it has to be done militarily, Britain will be there.'

So you were aware that this was the nature of the exchange at the very top level?

HOON: I wasn't aware of that specific exchange.

CHILCOT: We would like to ask some questions now on the legal dimension of the war, noting that you, yourself, are a professional lawyer by background, indeed a constitutional lawyer.

HOON: Not an international lawyer, though.

CHILCOT: That's true. Can we start almost a self-contained thing? In March 2002, your interview with Jonathan Dimbleby, you stated the view that the United Kingdom would be entitled to use the force without a specific United Nations Resolution.

Were you relying on your own view of the war in what you said to Jonathan Dimbleby?

HOON: I mean, this was a very wide-ranging interview. Let me put it this way: I was trying quite hard not to answer any questions, and that's quite difficult when there are only two of you having a conversation.

CHILCOT: So it shouldn't be understood – that's to say your Dimbleby interview moment – that that was a sort of settled and thought-through address to the situation as it was in March 2002 –

HOON: No –

CHILCOT: – in the real world?

HOON: I was trying pretty hard not to answer his questions in truth.

PRASHAR: You, yourself, have admitted that fatal errors in planning were made for the post-war. If you were alerted, did you inform the Prime Minister? Did you take any steps?

HOON: Of course. The initial situation on the ground was pretty good. I went to Iraq in April, after the invasion. I walked along the side of the Shatt al-Arab waterway. I talked to people. There were children following the soldiers around. They weren't following me, but they were fascinated by British soldiers. The soldiers were not wearing helmets, they were wearing berets. It was a very relaxed environment initially.

PRASHAR: There doesn't appear to be a single person within the Cabinet responsible for co-ordinating our approach to the aftermath.

HOON: I think that is probably a fair observation. I'm not retreating from that. But the local population quite quickly, perhaps understandably, blamed us for the problems that they had suffered for a long time under Saddam, and I'm not – it is not unreasonable, I can see why. They thought that we were there to help and we weren't making their lives any better as quickly as they expected. But no one in central government was actually saying, 'These are the issues. We need to take charge of this'.

LYNE: But the picture that has certainly been built up by a succession of military witnesses, is that, effectively, we had to make this up as we went along, that our military found themselves in charge of the civil administration of the south-east of Iraq for which they had not been prepared.

HOON: There was planning.

LYNE: Such planning as there was didn't produce the results?

HOON: Didn't deliver, no.

LYNE: Could that have been because the planning only started very late?

HOON: I think that's probably fair.

FREEDMAN: Lord Boyce said that he was forbidden to talk to the Chief of Defence [Logistics] because the government was not prepared to move forward on this. Is that correct?

HOON: The emphasis on the diplomatic process in September was paramount. At the same time, I and Lord Boyce – we both went to meetings in Downing Street saying, 'Look, you have got to get on with this', equally we were told in a sense, 'Calm down, we can't get on with it whilst the diplomatic process is underway' – we were both made very well aware of the attitude in Downing Street towards the requirement for minimising publicity and for avoiding the visibility of preparations. So there was no doubt of the fact that we could not go out, either of us, and overtly prepare.

FREEDMAN: In a sense covert rather than overt?

HOON: I think the judgment that I had to make and he had to make was the extent to which we could go on with preparations without affecting that diplomatic process in the United Nations.

FREEDMAN: So nonetheless, at this point, the view from Downing Street was that the political gain of the UN Resolution should not be put in jeopardy by overt military preparations.

HOON: The question of reserves of securing shipping, I mean, once you get to the stage of booking space on ships to transport tanks and other heavy equipment, it is pretty clear what you are up to.

FREEDMAN: So you saw that as politically sensitive --

HOON: Exactly.

FREEDMAN: The actual operation itself justified the confidence of the armed forces.

HOON: There were certainly some complaints about desert combats.

FREEDMAN: But I mean, if we just look at this question of clothing, we can look at boots as well, which was a related issue. I think the figure was that only 40 per cent of what was needed was available in theatre by 13 April a month after the invasion.

HOON: 40 per cent of what?

FREEDMAN: Of the extra boots and clothing.

HOON: I don't – What I don't know is – boots were more important than clothing in the sense that I recognise that in hot conditions having appropriate kind of desert boots is important.

FREEDMAN: Obviously, boots were the cause – always are a cause of particular irritation, but if your boots melt in the sun, it is not a small matter. Body armour. What was the problem with body armour?

HOON: It is not the kind of equipment which, up until then, had been routinely issued to British soldiers.

LYNE: As you go through to the spring of 2004, you really start to get a big rise in the level of violence and the beginnings of the Shia insurgency there.

FREEDMAN: Now, can we just look at these particular questions of helicopters? It is a critical resource.

HOON: I think that military commanders on the ground, rightly, and understandably, always want more equipment and I don't think anybody would doubt that.

FREEDMAN: But the lack of helicopters meant that it was – the forces were much more dependent on using the roads.

HOON: Yes.

FREEDMAN: Now, you have mentioned that the IED [improvised explosive devices] problem was not –

HOON: I have simply said it wasn't as great. I'm not minimising it.

FREEDMAN: It grew, I think was the point. This is one reason why the forces were so reliant on Snatch Land Rovers.

HOON: That's right, yes, but again, I mean part of the ethos and a more recent tradition of the British army is to get out amongst the local population, to interact with them, to be seen, not to be hidden in very heavily protected vehicles.

FREEDMAN: I mean, the consequence of relying on Snatch Land Rovers, because there wasn't really much else that could be used, was that – as a single source of British deaths, this is one of the most substantial – was this concern brought to your attention?

HOON: I think it was beginning to develop at the time that I left the department, yes.

ROSE: Gordon couldn't even tell you where Iraq was. He'd
never heard of it, not a clue. I don't think he really thought
he'd end up in a war.

He had a baby face did Gordon – always did, with a bit
of cheek. We used to call him fridge because he was six
foot four and ate everything in sight. Sandwiches, crisps,
snickers, sausage n' chips – you name it.

He left the day before my fortieth birthday. The hair was
gelled, trousers had to be spot on, shirt had to be spot on;
everything had to be perfect. Me, daughter and all his pals
from Pollok took him to the station. I felt butterflies in my
stomach and as he jumped on the train I said to Pamela
'he's not coming back'.

PETER: Shaun just made our marriage. It just does your first
son. The army was something he was always going to do.
I've got a picture of him at two years old, sitting on my
brother's knee with an army hat on.

It was one o'clock in the morning on Mother's Day when
we got a knock at the door. When you open your door at
that time to a bloke in uniform, you've got a good idea
what's happened.

ROSE: Two men came to my work. They took me into their
car, they were in the front and I was in the back. I asked
'what's he done? Has he fallen and broken a leg? He's a
bugger for climbing things!' Then the major said 'There's
no way of telling you. Gordon was killed this morning'. I
couldn't speak. I couldn't register what they were saying to
me.

We had to wait two weeks before we got him home.

PETER: You sort of go into autopilot. You are numb. Your kids
don't die before you.

The first thing we had to think about was Shaun coming home. We went down to Brize Norton. The aeroplane landed at midday and they brought thirteen coffins to the mortuary.

There were a lot of families, yeah. We had half an hour with Shaun. Luckily he wasn't badly damaged so we could see him one last time. One lady had a problem where two or three soldiers were blown up so the MOD scraped them all together and said right, there's an arm and there's a leg.

ROSE: The night before the funeral, I slept in the chair next to him. And in that front room, I made him a promise. I said I'm not letting this go Gordon. I'll find out why you were killed.

It took five years before we got the inquest. They cancelled it four times. So I founded Military Families Against War, I stood for Parliament and the more the MOD mucked me around, the angrier I would get. At one point somebody from the press phoned up and said 'Rose the MOD are trying to put a gagging order on you' and I said 'They can't do nothing else to me can they? Let them gag me. I've got two daughters here and we're not going to leave it.' I promised Gordon.

PETER: My son died because nobody knew how to adequately fit equipment onto his vehicle.

ROSE: The inquest concluded it was a breakdown of the chain of command and unlawful killing. I knew it, I just needed to hear it

The armour that the Land Rover needed to protect Gordon from the roadside bomb had never been fitted. It was locked in a storeroom for five months 800 yards away from him. Between emails getting deleted, the army never passed the information on.

That armour was meant to get fitted an hour after Gordon got killed.

PETER: There is a metal plate that fits on the front of all army vehicles. A helicopter is supposed to fire a laser signal down to hit that plate which then reflects in the dark. It's basically thermal imaging. But the army didn't know how to fit it so they stuck the plate on the wrong headlight. This meant that when there was debris on the road at night, Shaun couldn't see. The Land Rover he was driving overturned. Shaun died in the ambulance on the way to camp.

ROSE: I've been following Chilcot. I don't think we are going to get the answers. It's been going on too long. I knew Tony Blair's lies. His total lies. I mean they still can't prove to this day why we went into Iraq. I said that from the beginning if Gordon had put another uniform on and got killed in another war I'd have to accept that. But not for Iraq. Definitely not for Iraq.

PETER: Shaun drives me on. I campaign to keep his name alive. I didn't want him to be a number. I wanted his name, it had to be his name.

My wife and the kids even will say 'you've never grieved' and I don't want to grieve. I want to make it right.

My son died believing he was protecting his country, but he died for Tony Blair's legacy. I need Chilcot to find out all about the lies and to find out the truth about what happened in Iraq. Until then I can't move on.

ROSE: When I finally cleared Gordon's room, it just looked bare. I thought no, I'm going to have to put my bed into his room. It felt like I was closer to him again. One thing I did keep was his bottle of Jeep aftershave. That was his favourite. I used to say 'Gordon you smell like a whore's handbag' but I still spray it now and then. Everywhere. Because it makes me laugh and I can still smell him. It reminds me of him.

PETER: My son was killed on the 30 March on the Kuwait Border. His name is Shaun Andrew Brierley.

ROSE: My son was Gordon Gentle who was nineteen. He was killed in Basra in Iraq, 2004.

Blackout.

<u>*Evidence of Witness Tony Blair to the Chilcot Inquiry (29 January 2010 and 21 Jan 2011)*</u>

CHILCOT: Good morning everyone. Today the Iraq Inquiry will be hearing from the Rt Hon Tony Blair, the Prime Minister until June 2007. Good morning.

BLAIR: Good morning.

GILBERT: Mr Blair, the very powerful speech you made to the House of Commons on 18 March 2003 was of critical importance. Without Parliament's approval our troops would not have been able to participate in the invasion. In your speech you drew an analogy with the 1930s, the moment you said when Czechoslovakia was swallowed up by the Nazis. That's when we should have acted. This was not the first time that analogy had been made.

Comparing Iraq with Nazi Germany has enormous emotive force with the British public. It also heightens perceptions of the level and imminence of the threat. In your book *A Journey* you say that you regretted and almost took out that reference. Can you tell us why?

BLAIR: Let me just make one thing very clear, I don't regret the basic point I am making. My view after September 11 was that our whole analysis of the terrorist threat and extremism had to change. The single most important thing to me about September 11 is that 3,000 people died, but if they could have killed 30,000, they would have. Where I think the analogy is valid is in supposing we just let Saddam carry on, would it really have been such a problem? My anxiety is that yes, we cannot take that risk.

There are two views in this world. One view is that extremism is an encrustment on an otherwise manageable situation. Don't over-worry about it. Don't provoke it. Don't stimulate it. Just manage the situation. The other view, which is my view, is that this thing is deep. Its potential to wreak enormous and devastating damage is huge and we have to confront it.

Now if that is an echo of how people were dealing with fascism in the 1930s that is the echo.

FREEDMAN: Let me just sum up where it seems to me that as February (2003) was turning into March. There hasn't been a real find of chemical or biological stocks. The inspectors were not saying that they couldn't do their job. There was no nuclear programme. Was this not a good time to take stock and to question whether or not more time would have been helpful?

BLAIR: I think there was a judgment being made – that, you know, more time was not going to solve this.

PRASHAR: Lord Boyce [Chief of Defence Staff] and Mr Hoon [Defence Secretary] have spoken about the restrictions placed on the visible military preparations in December 2002.

BLAIR: Geoff Hoon said to me, 'We have really got to get on with this now'. The UK military got on with it, and they did it magnificently, as they always do.

PRASHAR: That's true, but there was no visible preparedness, and things like the provision of essential kit, medical supplies, combat boots, body armour – very important in a situation where there could be a threat of nuclear, biological and chemical weapons – protection clothing, ammunition. As it happened, the kit did not arrive until late and that was the case.

BLAIR: All I know is that they regarded themselves as ready.

PRASHAR: Why were you reluctant to have any visible preparation?

BLAIR: Well, we changed and we did have the visible preparation.

PRASHAR: But that came late, that's my point.

BLAIR: We were anxious to make sure people did not think there was an inevitability about this.

LYNE: Can you identify a point before March 2003 at which you specifically sought a decision from the Cabinet?

BLAIR: The issue was being canvassed in the Cabinet in the sense that the facts weren't really in dispute.

LYNE: But our military preparations were being made in great secrecy?

BLAIR: That's necessary frankly.

LYNE: Do you think it was clear, do you think it was understood within the Cabinet that we actually had military preparations underway?

BLAIR: It really does defy common sense and logic, let alone the discussion, to think that there were people in the Cabinet who didn't know what was – that we were on a course where the principles of it were absolutely clear. Go down the UN route, get an ultimatum. If Saddam fails to meet the ultimatum we are going to be with America on military action. I sent it out with crystal clarity.

The thing was throughout, and this is why I go back to September 11, my view was I was not oblivious to the difficulties, but in the end were we going to stand firm and deal with this threat alongside America or not? That was the issue. You know, you can go round this 1,000 times but you come back to that same basic challenge.

LYNE: Just to say, Mr Blair, we have checked or rechecked the Cabinet records between April and September of 2002 and the records show that there wasn't a substantive discussion of Iraq in that period. The subject came up twice.

BLAIR: Does that include the period of the recess, by the way?

LYNE: The period I was referring to was between April and September (2002).

LYNE: On 15 January 2003 you told the House of Commons there are circumstances in which a second UN resolution is not necessary. Now Lord Goldsmith has said in his statement to us that these words of yours were not compatible with the advice that he had given to you the day before. Did you understand at the time that your words were inconsistent with the legal advice?

BLAIR: I was making basically a political point. However, I accept entirely that there was an inconsistency between what he was saying and what I was saying there.

CHILCOT: I think we would like to pursue the Al Qaeda point, if we may. It is really one for Sir Roderic Lyne. Rod.

LYNE: Given that we had by this stage been engaged with the United States for two years in a global war on terror, as President Bush called it, and we were about to invade and occupy an Islamic country with a substantial Sunni population, shouldn't the experts have anticipated – I am wary of hindsight – that Al Qaeda would seek to exploit such a situation against us?

BLAIR: I am out in the Middle East a lot of the time now and it's the same issue everywhere. What happened when you got Al Qaeda coming into this situation is that it was more than just a few terrorists. It was backed with an ideology that said the west is fundamentally hostile to Islam and that's why we have to wage war against these people.

LYNE: As you rightly say they came into a situation that was very fertile ground for them. Looting started almost immediately. The invading and then occupying forces were not able to ensure law and order. Even arms dumps were not guarded. We had, of course, dismantled the regime self-evidently, but we had in the course of doing that – we went on to dismantle much of the public service through de-Ba'athification. As a result of this post-conflict situation in what was already a fragile and unstable country a power vacuum developed. That was where our preparations went wrong?

BLAIR: I think there is something in that but I think you can make far too much of it. I don't think that Al Qaeda stepped into a power vacuum. They simply need people who are prepared to go and blow themselves up in a street market. When that happens, you destabilise the country. That's the purpose of it. That is why it's such a frightening phenomenon, I am afraid, all over.

LYNE: I think nobody is disputing how unpleasant or ruthless Al Qaeda is. Of course, the majority of the people who made Iraq virtually unmanageable were Iraqis. They were internal. They came from different groups. Not all of the extremists were Al Qaeda by any means. In fact, almost every group in the struggle for power had extremist elements in it and, indeed, still does to this day, as we see from the pattern of continuing terrorism that goes on.

PRASHAR: I now want to turn to the aftermath planning. In January 2003, you said: 'We cannot engage in military conflict and ignore the aftermath'. Now, what happened? Because you know, this was inadequate and a lot of people have said it didn't quite work.

BLAIR: We had the ad hoc meetings, we had Cabinet meetings, actually, that were discussing these issues. The real problem was that we planned for certain eventualities but we discovered a different set of realities.

PRASHAR: I mean, were you aware that we would assume responsibilities as an occupying power under the Geneva and Hague Conventions? Why did we accept the status of a joint occupying power?

BLAIR: Because we were the key partner of the US in this. We believed in it and we were prepared to accept the responsibility of putting the country right.

PRASHAR: Did we actually weigh up all the liability, the risks and the implications, the resources required?

BLAIR: Absolutely, and one of the things that we could not walk away from our commitment to people in Iraq afterwards.

PRASHAR: It is the adequacy of the planning on a whole range of things, economic, political, because in a way there was a danger, there was information that Iraq could have fractured, given the insecurity of the Kurds, what could have happened with the Shias and Sunnis. I mean, there is a whole range of eventualities which you planned for that wasn't done.

BLAIR: I would say we most certainly did plan for the problems in relation to the potential for a Sunni/Shia/Kurd split.

The trouble was we didn't plan for two things: one was, as I say, the absence of this properly functioning Civil Service infrastructure; and, of course, the second thing, which is people did not think that Al-Qaeda and Iran would play the role that they did. This in my view is a huge lesson.

FREEDMAN: In April 2004, which was the revelation of what happened at Abu Ghraib, what was your reaction when you saw the photographs of the conditions inside the prison?

BLAIR: Well, I was shocked and angry, as anyone would be.

FREEDMAN: The year after the invasion I just want to give you some figures, because I find them tragic. We are in January 2010 now. These are just January monthly figures, the documented civilian deaths from violence in Iraq. 570 in January 2004, 1,042 in January 2005, 1,433 in January 2006. 2,807 in January 2007. The striking thing is they are getting worse each year. What could you say to the Iraqi people that could explain what they must have felt the coalition had done for them?

BLAIR: The coalition forces weren't the ones doing the killing. The ones doing the killing were the terrorists, the sectarians, and they were doing it quite deliberately to stop us making the progress we wanted to make. The situation in Iraq today is very, very different.

FREEDMAN: Let us hope so.

CHILCOT: There is gratitude, great gratitude, to our armed forces for the sacrifices they made and the bravery they showed and great sorrow at their losses. But we, like you, have also experienced at first hand the anger which is still felt by many people in this country and we have been asking, the question why. And so, as we conclude today, can I ask what broad lessons you have drawn and regrets?

BLAIR: I feel – of course, I had to take this decision as Prime Minister and it was a huge responsibility then, and there is not a single day that passes by that I don't reflect and think about that responsibility. In the end it was divisive, and I'm sorry about that, but if I'm asked whether I believe we are safer, more secure, that Iraq is better, our own security is better with Saddam and his two sons out of power I think we live in a completely new security environment today.

I indeed believe that in time to come, if Iraq becomes the country that its people want to see, then we can look back, and particularly our armed forces can look back, with an immense sense of pride and achievement in what they did.

CHILCOT: And no regrets?

BLAIR: Responsibility, but not regret for removing Saddam Hussein. I think that he was a monster, I believe he threatened, not just the region but the world. I do genuinely believe that the world is safer and I really think it is time we learned, as a matter of sensible foreign policy, that the way to deal with one dictatorial threat is not to back another.

INTERVIEW 5 – ALI

ALI: When the invasion took place the British were in control of the South Basra area. After the occupation, the coalition appointed a government. The government was quasi-Iranian and started talking in a sectarian manner. Then a large number of Shia militias took control of Basra. They started killing the professionals as well as the leaders of the Sunni society, from scholars to the tribal leaders. And they started generally killing the Sunni, they killed on identity. Just by showing your ID card, they knew what you are and they killed you. It's as simple as that.

On the 12 September 2013 we were praying in the Mosque in Zubair. I was actually praying in a Sunni mosque, but I was not praying in a Sunni area so they were lying in wait. They kidnapped me with some other young men, between 4 and 4.30 in the afternoon. When we left there were cars that had Shia militias, between five and six cars. Not ordinary cars by the way, they are special vehicles. Everybody knows they are militia. They were all dressed in black and they had green ribbons on their foreheads with the writing that they are militia. Their faces were covered except for their eyes. They were carrying handguns with silencers on. I felt they were going to kill me immediately. It is known and it is a fact that normally when the militia kidnap people they kill them immediately.

They hit us on the back of our heads and put us in the backs of their trucks and went on beating us during the journey. As soon as they put us in our cars they blindfolded us. They beat us up until we reached their headquarters. They put us in this room. They removed our blindfolds. We could see the whole place was bloody. The floor was covered in blood. This room was specifically used for torture.

Afterwards they started beating us and then they peed on us.

It's a very large white long sort of knife.

Like a chopping…

It's very sharp.

And they tried to chop my knee off.

I started bleeding.

I realized that we were about to die.

The only thing I did was say the Sahaba because for Muslims before they die they say the Sahaba. That is the only thing I've got: – I bear witness that there is no God other than God. And I bear witness that there is no God other than Allah.

I fainted when they burnt me, when they burnt me with petrol. They poured kerosene on me and left me for dead. I was found by the local council and they contacted the ambulance set-up in Basra and they picked me up.

Then my family took me to a private hospital to be treated so I stayed there. When they used to bathe me I could not look at my body. I just used to cry. I remained in hospital for another six or seven months.

In my nightmares I see them killing me. I see them killing me over and over again. I always think about this in my daylight hours, in my waking hours. What is it that I have done? What is our fault? What is it we have committed? Why this torture? What is the use of all this torture? What is the good of all this torture? None of us understand. The only people who know are the militias who commit these sorts of acts.

My life was turned upside down by the occupation of Iraq. After the occupation, Basra was handed over to the militias. It was handed over to the militias because the British couldn't control the situation.

It was all about death. Daily there is death. I do not believe that Iraq has any future.

LYNE: Mr Campbell, good morning. You worked for Mr Blair from 1994 until you announced your resignation on 29 August 2003. You were the Prime Minister's director of communications and strategy. That's a very broad job description. What was your actual role?

CAMPBELL: My job was to work to help devise and implement communication strategies for the government and the Prime Minister.

LYNE: You have said that you, basically, were there to do whatever the Prime Minister asked you to do. Would that be accurate?

CAMPBELL: Look, if he asked me to jump off a building, I wouldn't have done it.

LYNE: Being serious.

CAMPBELL: I talked earlier about the changing nature of the media, it has had a significant impact upon policymaking. My job was to try to advise him through some of the tricky currents that that threw up.

LYNE: You told the [Commons] Foreign Affairs Committee: 'I was involved in a lot of the discussions about policy and strategy on Iraq'...

CAMPBELL: Well, I was.

LYNE: So surely you were a policy person?

CAMPBELL: Yes, thinking the whole time about communications issues.

LYNE: [Moving to] the Prime Minister's working methods, would he, from time to time, assemble close advisers as a group, when he was wrestling with issues on Iraq? Would he get you all together or would he talk to you individually? Would it happen almost ad hoc? How did it work?

CAMPBELL: I would be phoned at the weekend and I would know he would be phoning other people as well. He would be having lots of conversations. Most Mondays, he sent a note out to what you would call his inner circle. When you got on to meetings specifically to do with Iraq, from memory, the people who would almost certainly be at those would be Jack Straw, Geoff Hoon, Admiral Boyce, John Scarlett [MI6], sometimes Richard Dearlove [MI6] and myself.

CHILCOT: Could you slow that down because of the stenographer?

CAMPBELL: Sorry:

LYNE: Quoting from the Crawford press conference [in Texas April 2002], you had the Prime Minister say 'All the options available will be considered.' Now, can you recall from all of these meetings that were held on Iraq in 2001/2002 what meetings the Prime Minister did hold to consider all of the strategic options and the likely consequences of each?

CAMPBELL: How many meetings did the Prime Minister hold on Iraq? Dozens and dozens and dozens.

LYNE: What were those strategic options?

CAMPBELL: The Prime Minister's overall approach was saying, ultimately, there is going to be disarmament. We are going to do our level best to get that done through the diplomatic route without a single shot being fired, but if push comes to shove and the diplomatic route fails, Britain would see it as its responsibility and its duty to take part in military action.

LYNE: Presumably the Prime Minister wrote to President Bush from time to time. Did you see that correspondence?

CAMPBELL: Yes.

LYNE: Did he tell President Bush in writing during 2002 that he would support the President if he took military action?

CAMPBELL: The Prime Minister wrote quite a lot of notes to the President and I would say that the tenor of them was that we share the analysis, we share the concern, we are absolutely with you in making sure that Saddam Hussein is faced up to his obligations and that Iraq is disarmed. If that can't be done diplomatically and it has to be done militarily, Britain will be there.

LYNE: So without conditions?

CAMPBELL: It is not a question of being without conditions, because if you are saying that along that route –

LYNE: Let's not go all the way along the route.

CAMPBELL: You have just asked me the question. If I can answer it: twelve years after the first UN resolution, six months after George Bush takes it to the United Nations, four months after Security Council Resolution 1441 – I think the Prime Minister was, all the way through, trying to get it resolved without a single shot being fired. That was his motivation right the way through.

LYNE: A couple of points about the letters between the Prime Minister and President Bush that you referred to. Would these letters have been drafted by others?

CAMPBELL: I think they were pretty private.

LYNE: You saw them? Who else would have seen them?

CAMPBELL: I don't know is the short answer to that.

LYNE: The Foreign Secretary?

CAMPBELL: I would have thought so, yes.

LYNE: The Defence Secretary?

CAMPBELL: I think it would depend. They were very frank.

49

LYNE: Very frank and advisory? Thank you.

FREEDMAN: Why was a [Iraq weapons dossier] perceived to be necessary in September 2002?

CAMPBELL: The dossier was seen to be necessary because the Prime Minister had been growing more and more concerned, post-September 11. Of course, what he saw was material that really only he and a number of other senior ministers were able to see. What he did want to do was to set out for the public, in as accessible a way as possible, the reasons why he had become more concerned.

FREEDMAN: So this very much then depended on the newness of the information, the revelatory nature of the document?

CAMPBELL: Partly, yes. Not wholly, but partly.

FREEDMAN: There had been two papers prepared before the Dossier was drafted. There had been one prepared by the Joint Intelligence Committee [JIC] in March 2002.

CAMPBELL: Yes.

FREEDMAN: Why was it decided not to use that paper there? There would have been one reason perhaps for caution on the February 2002 one, that, by looking at Iran, Libya, North Korea as well as Iraq, it would have brought home the fact that those other countries were actually further advanced and of greater concern in terms of nuclear weapons, than Iraq.

CAMPBELL: I think, were Tony Blair here, what he would say to that is – the reason why he was more concerned about Iraq was partly because they had used chemical weapons, partly because of the nature of the regime.

FREEDMAN: On 5 and 9 September [2002] you chaired two meetings in the Cabinet Office with senior officials, including John Scarlett [chairman of the Joint Intelligence Committee] and senior MI6 officers to discuss the dossier. Why were you chairing these meetings?

It was an unusual thing for you chairing a meeting of intelligence professionals, with intelligence professionals present?

CAMPBELL: I accept that.

FREEDMAN: There wasn't precedent, but the whole way through it could not have been made clearer to everybody that John Scarlett was the person who, if you like, had the single pen.

CAMPBELL: Yes.

FREEDMAN: You are trying to make a case.

CAMPBELL: I cannot stress strongly enough and I think this was very, very clear, that not a single [government official] at any time sought to question, override, rewrite, let alone the ghastly 'sex up' phrase, the intelligence assessments in any way, at any time, on any level.

FREEDMAN: You will be delighted to know I am now going to turn to the forty-five minutes' claim. Now, this has been a subject of great interest. It has been established that you didn't make up the claim and that you didn't insert it in the dossier.

CAMPBELL: It has been established, yes.

FREEDMAN: The key thing is that the Joint Intelligence Committee [JIC] stated that: 'Iraq has probably dispersed its special weapons. Intelligence also indicates that chemical and biological munitions could be with military units and ready for firing within twenty to forty-five minutes.'

I'm just wondering whether you or members of your team were involved in the discussion of how this forty-five minutes was going to be introduced.

CAMPBELL: It wasn't within the discussions. To be frank, it wasn't that big a deal. I have made two points on this. I mean, the original intelligence, as you say, says twenty to forty-five minutes. If we had been in the sexing up game, I think we would have said, 'Come on John, can't we do the twenty minutes rather than the forty-five?' That discussion never took place. So I don't think we were ever saying, 'Look, Saddam Hussein has got these weapons and he can whack them off the Cyprus in forty-five minutes,' and if one or two of the papers went down that line, they weren't pushed there by us. Could it have been clearer? Obviously.

FREEDMAN: I think Jonathan Powell [Mr Blair's chief of staff] sent you an email on 19 September: 'Alastair, what would be the headline in the Standard on the day of publication? What do we want it to be?' What did you want it to be?

CAMPBELL: What did I reply?

FREEDMAN: I don't know. When you saw, *Evening Standard*: 'forty-five minutes from attack. Iraqis could have a nuclear bomb in a year. There are some Brits forty-five minutes from doom … ' reference to Cyprus. *Express*: 'Saddam can strike in forty-five minutes.' Were you surprised by those headlines?

CAMPBELL: I'm not surprised by anything that most of the British newspapers write on a daily basis. I still – I defend every single word of the dossier, I defend every single part of the process, and I think it was an attempt by the Prime Minister to engage the public properly in trying to – in understanding why the Prime Minister's thinking was developing as it was.

GILBERT: On 15 February 2003, vast numbers of people, including two of my children walked through the streets of London protesting about the Iraq war. What account did you take of this strength of public opinion?

CAMPBELL: I always have a rule of thumb that, if somebody goes on a march, there are probably ten others who thought about it. The Prime Minister knew that this was a deeply unpopular and not just unpopular like tuition fees or whatever it might have been – this was deep.

But he is elected as the Prime Minister I saw how much it weighed upon him, but, equally, I saw somebody who fundamentally really deeply believed that, unless the world confronted Saddam Hussein there would be a bigger day of reckoning later on, and I think he still believes that now.

GILBERT: Was this moral case one that you were then able, in the short time that remained before the debate, to promulgate in some way through your efforts?

CAMPBELL: For heaven's sake, let's do away with all the conspiracy theories that it was about oil, it was about George Bush telling Tony Blair what to do. Somebody who has been elected Prime Minister and wants to get re-elected.

LYNE: On the question of the way that the Cabinet was involved in there was a remarkable absence of papers for these Cabinet discussions. Why weren't there papers for the discussions?

CAMPBELL: I don't know. My job was not preparing papers for Cabinet.

LYNE: Why wasn't the Secretary of State for International Development included in this inner circle of people, given that her department was going to be the lead department dealing with the aftermath of the conflict as well as with its humanitarian consequences?

CAMPBELL: That is a very good question, and I think, in an ideal world, the Secretary of State for International Development would, should, and could, have been in all of those discussions.

LYNE: Are you implying in your deeply diplomatic way that the Secretary of State for International Development was not regarded as trustworthy or as competent?

CAMPBELL: When Clare Short and her department were in support of a Government policy or position, then I think she was both trustworthy and competent.

LYNE: Because she was difficult, her department couldn't therefore be included fully in the work. What were the consequences of this for the Government's ability to plan effectively for the aftermath of the conflict?

CAMPBELL: Again, I'm not an expert on that side of Government policy and planning, but would it have helped to have had better relations? Almost certainly.

LYNE: It certainly didn't help. Looking at the huge cost in loss of life over, now, six and a half years, at the effects on the stability of the Middle Eastern region, at the development of international terrorism within Iraq, do you consider that, overall, the policy has succeeded?

CAMPBELL: I do. The death toll has been high in terms of Iraqis, and obviously any loss of any British soldier's life is not just tragic but it obviously weighs heavily on anybody who was involved in that process, most particularly, obviously, the Prime Minister.

CHILCOT: I think we have pretty much come to the end of this session. My question to you, Mr Campbell: have we given you sufficient opportunity to offer us your reflections on the lessons to be learned, real world lessons, from that whole experience?

CAMPBELL: Real world?

CHILCOT: Real world lessons.

CAMPBELL: The only thing I would say is you can have all the advisers you want, whether it is people like me, diplomats or the military, but ultimately the guys who are elected, at the top, they do finally have to make decisions. I hope that, as a result of remaining divisions over the policy on Iraq, that we don't put a future generation of leaders in a position where the really, really, really difficult decisions can't be taken.

Evidence of Witness Clare Short to the Chilcot Inquiry
(2 February 2010)

CHILCOT: Good morning and welcome to everyone, and welcome to our witness. The objective of this session is to hear from Clare Short, who was Secretary of State for International Development from 1997 until May 2003, when you resigned over the Iraq question.

GILBERT: We asked Mr Blair whether a new Iraq policy had been discussed in Cabinet. He replied it had not, but he went on to tell us: 'The discussion we had in Cabinet was substantive.' Do you recall such a discussion and what was your contribution to it?

SHORT: The Cabinet didn't work in the way that, according to our constitutional theory, it is supposed to work. I mean, the meetings were very short. There were never papers. There were little chats about things, but it wasn't a decision-making body in any serious way and I don't remember at all Iraq coming to the Cabinet. It became a sofa government. If ever you raised an issue that you wanted to bring to the Cabinet, Tony Blair would see you beforehand and cut it off, saying 'we don't want those things coming to the Cabinet' which he did to me. There was stuff in press about Iraq and I said, 'I really think we should have a discussion about Iraq' and he said, 'I do not want us to because it might leak into the press'.

LYNE: I would like to go back into the machinery of government that you mentioned.

SHORT: It is partly the twenty-four-hour news thing. Power is pulled into Number 10. The House of Commons is now a rubber stamp, it doesn't scrutinise. In the case of Iraq, there was secretiveness and deception on top of that.

LYNE: Sorry, who misled the Cabinet? The Attorney General?

SHORT: I think for the Attorney General to come and say there is an unequivocal legal authority to go to war was misleading.

LYNE: Lord Goldsmith has denied that he acted under pressure. Now, do you accept what he and Mr Blair have said about this?

SHORT: I am afraid I don't. I do not have any evidence, but I think him changing his mind three times in a couple of weeks and then even – in order to say unequivocally there was legal authority to require Tony Blair to secretly sign a document saying that Iraq was in material breach [of his disarmament obligations] and not to report any of that to the Cabinet is so extraordinary.

There was no evidence of any kind of an escalation of threat. So there was no hurry. I mean, that's one of the kinds of untruths, the exaggeration, of the risk of [weapons of mass destruction].

LYNE: Was it a question that we had to take military action to topple Saddam?

SHORT: I'm saying we could have gone more slowly and carefully and not had a totally destabilised Iraq into which came Al-Qaeda that wasn't there before, and that Tony Blair account of the need to act urgently somehow, because of September 11, does not stack up to any scrutiny whatsoever. We have made Iraq more dangerous as well as causing enormous suffering.

LYNE: So you think there were alternative ways other than toppling Saddam Hussein, of preventing him from becoming a more serious threat?

SHORT: As I have said, Saudi Arabia and Jordan were talking about getting him into exile. There was the possibility of the International Criminal Court.

FREEDMAN: Did you discuss this with other Cabinet colleagues at the time?

SHORT: No, things were enormously fraught. I had various cups of coffee with Gordon [Brown] and discussed with him – and he was very unhappy and marginalised. He was worried about other things beyond Iraq. He would say on Iraq, 'We must uphold the UN', and I would say, 'I agree, but are we going to do it that way?' and then he would talk about other issues that were worrying him and I would rabbit on about Iraq. So I'm not sure we were communicating terribly fully, but we were having cups of coffee.

I didn't know Robin [Cook] was going to resign. You can see how poor the communication – well, the discussion in the Cabinet was. It was Tony Blair told me, when he called me in to see him privately, and said, 'Robin has gone – going today'.

PRASHAR: Talking about the aftermath planning on the eve of the invasion, because you were raising all these issues, you were not being listened to. Why did you continue to support the policy?

SHORT: Do you mean why didn't I resign?

PRASHAR: Yes.

SHORT: I have tried to answer that. If I knew then what I know now, I would have. But I had the Prime Minister getting the President of the United States to agree to the publication of the [Middle East] road map, which should have meant a Palestinian state by the end of 2005 – think how that would have transformed the Middle East – and I had the Prime Minister of Britain promising me that he had got Bush to agree that there would be a UN lead on reconstruction.

I was conned. I agreed with the policy as it was formally stated. I just don't think that was the policy. We were just in a bit of a lunatic asylum.

GILBERT: What was the relationship, once DFID [the department for international development] personnel were in south Iraq with the military? How did that relationship affect your effectiveness?

SHORT: We had always had good relationships with the military, because we are can-doers and so are they. Of course, in this case it was totally different because we had been frozen out. I think that affected my relationship with [Admiral] Boyce [chief of the defence staff]. As people used to say, he'd spent a lot of his life in submarines and it showed. He wasn't a chatty sort of chap, and – I would go in each day and say, 'This is happening in Basra, this disorder, this electricity', it really annoyed him. He wasn't getting those kinds of reports.

LYNE: You say that we should have allowed more time, we should have done it all through the UN, and I think you said earlier that the Russians, the French and the Germans were essentially saying that they would be prepared to agree to military action but not at this time. But we have heard the argument from Jack Straw and Tony Blair that President Chirac had said in his broadcast on 10 March [2003] that they weren't going to agree in any circumstances.

SHORT: That was – in my view – that was a lie, a deliberate lie. At that point – if you remember – Blair, he was grey and thin and under enormous strain at the failure of the second resolution. At that point John Prescott brought Gordon Brown and him together, Gordon came in, and the strategy was: blame the French and claim that they'd said they would veto anything.

CHILCOT: This Inquiry has got two basic tasks, I think, to fulfil. The first is to establish a reliable account of what happened from many people's different perspectives, and the other, of course, is to identify serious lessons to be learned from that whole experience. I would invite you to give any comments you have with that in mind, by way of final remarks today.

SHORT: About the special relationship. We really need a serious debate in our country about what we mean by it, whether it is unconditional poodle-like adoration and do whatever America says. I think we have ended up humiliating ourselves.

I think, as I have said, the machinery of government has broken down quite badly – and is focused on announcing things endlessly to the media. The House of Commons is now so powerless, it is a rubber stamp. Too much legislation. Policy is not properly thought through. When you add secrecy and deceit, the system becomes positively dangerous. I'm still shocked that Britain could do what happened in Iraq and it makes me fear for our government system.

SHAIKH MARWAN AL DULAIMI: I am head of my tribe and
I am a chief in the Iraqi Revolutionary Tribal Council.
Before 2003 I used to run my father's business in
construction work. My father used to adjudicate all the
tribal conflicts.

I wanted to be a revolutionary because I could see Iraq
being torn apart in front of my eyes. The Americans used
to throw leaflets from the planes, showering us with leaflets
saying that we are going to have all the food products that
you could imagine. At the time of sanctions and embargo
we only had twelve food products but the American
government was going to introduce forty-three items –
including soft drinks. Lovely.

The Iraqi people waited for six months patiently to
see what the invading forces were going to do. There
was planes bombing from the skies and artillery in the
desert. They started ploughing out the orchards and
bringing down the houses. We were out in the wild,
outside Baghdad. From my tribe 380 were killed by the
Americans. It was very difficult. I lost some good friends.

There was an incident 1,000 metres away from my home.
There is a field where young girls in their teens normally
cut grass to take for cows because they live off milking
cows and selling milk and butter and so on. The American
troops once came and just shot all the girls alleging they
were resistance. Three. Just like that. I knew them. These
girls were from my tribe. This means that they are family.

When people came to pay their condolences they all said
we must fight the invaders. Women took off their head-
dress and said they will not wear it again until they have
taken their revenge. The tribes had no other choice but to
fight. We became incubating system for the resistance.

That night we attacked an American convoy. There were two large American army trucks with four smaller ones. The tribes in the area are all connected by one road and the American habit was that they would move from one tribe to the other using the same road.

There was a firefight. Each resistance group in each tribe communicated with each other on the telecommunications. We had these large telephones, giving each other information about where the Americans were. So as the convoy moved along the road and escape one tribe, they don't escape the next.

When we killed thirty the resistance was very happy. It's all a matter of vengeance. I will not tell you whether or not I held a gun. But did the resistance feel remorse? No remorse, never. An invader should expect this. Does the occupier feel remorse when they kill our children? Do they feel remorse when we are tortured? Are they happy causing the death of two million people?

All tribes are made up of former army officers, doctors, engineers, everything that you can imagine. Their loyalty is to the tribe and they all came back to the tribe. I helped them to buy arms to set up these groups. And we are growing. When someone gets killed fighting, we look after their families, their children. The stupidity of the American and British army and their policy in Iraq helped us grow. Every time they detained 100 people due to supposed 'information', 1,000 people join the resistance.

The government is a tool of the occupation. They started saying that our resistance is Al-Qaeda or the former Baath party – any label. They would just not admit we are a real tribal insurgency, a true insurgency from the people of Iraq.

We are not radicalized. I am against radicalization. I didn't go to London, I didn't go to Paris or Brussels, I didn't go anywhere. I was sitting in my own home when the invaders came and behaved as if they owned the place. We are tribes and we have customs and habits and principles. We need these back. We need Iraq to be free.

Evidence given in Private from MI6 Witness to the Chilcot Inquiry

GILBERT: This session is being held in private because we recognise much of the evidence on the areas we want to cover will be sensitive. [This morning we will be hearing from a witness from MI6] To open up the questions, what was the plan for the post-conflict search for WMD?

MI6(3): Initially, I assumed, as others did, that there was indeed WMD. But obviously, [it] became clear within a few weeks there was a problem. We had expected to come across facilities or shells and so on, and we didn't. Therefore there was already political clamour, if you like.

We withdrew the intelligence, I think very quickly. It was obvious that this was not a good case.

LYNE: What I want to know is how it had gone to the Prime Minister and whether your usual procedures for checking intelligence before you put it to a very high level had been followed in this case.

MI6(3): No. I had no direct knowledge of what had happened previously.

LYNE: When you looked into the case, discovered that it wasn't valid, what conclusions do you recall drawing about this case as a whole?

MI6(3): The point is that when you have senior people who reach down into the machinery and try moving the cogs, if I may put it like that, I think you end up with a – you obviously disenfranchise the operational chain of command.

You cut out expertise, and perhaps you also disable that element of challenge which is, I think, a very important part of operational life in [MI6]. There was a judgment that we had over-promised and under-delivered. I absolutely agreed with that judgment. It's precisely what we did.

LYNE: Thank you. What were the pressures – were they political pressures, for example – that caused your very professional service, with years of experience behind it, not to be as careful as it should have been over a source of this kind, an unvalidated, untested source?

MI6(3): Clearly when you are under a lot of pressure to produce intelligence, there is a risk that you will take short cuts.

LYNE: Had the Chief [Dearlove] got too close to the Prime Minister?

MI6(3): I was not in a position to observe. But I think the issue was that – I mean, it soon became an issue that there was a public portrayal, if you like, of senior intelligence officers, a public portrayal of them as Whitehall courtiers, and I think that was damaging externally in relation to the reputation of the Service for professionalism, and furthermore damaging – particularly with younger officers in the Service, damaging for their sense of intellectual integrity.

LYNE: Thank you.

MI6(3): Meanwhile, actually, we had, you know, the start of a major insurgency.

CHILCOT: Yes.

MI6(3): And the point was that from, I would say, about the middle of 2004, the Sunnis just didn't recognise what their own interests were. That is to say they were taking on the Americans. Obviously they strongly resented the Shia taking over the state, although the Sunnis never really accepted that they were only sort of 30 per cent of the population, and they of course had always dominated – when I say 'always', actually I mean pretty much always – dominated the political system. The Sunni felt that they had had the state stolen away from them. So their immediate reaction, of course, was to fight. I felt that here we were in a democracy without democrats.

If you look at it at a human level, I think it's important to understand how individuals reacted to what became clear was highly oppressive behaviour by the Shia authorities, intermingled obviously with their militias, and come 2005/2006, some really bad things were going on. If your relatives had been detained, brutalised, perhaps killed by those authorities or that militia, then you were going to join Al Qaeda or do anything to take revenge.

Evidence of Witness Eliza Manningham-Buller, former head of MI5 to the Chilcot Inquiry (20 July 2010)

CHILCOT: Good morning and welcome everyone, and welcome to our witness, Baroness Manningham-Buller, Director General of the Security Service [MI5] from 2002 to 2007.

In your judgment [was] the effect of the invasion of Iraq to substantially increase the terrorist threat to the United Kingdom?

MB: I think because of evidence of the number of plots, the number of leads, the number of people identified, and statements of people as to why they were involved, I think the answer to your question [is] yes.

PRASHAR: I think it would be very helpful if you would give us a very quick resume of how the Security Service was involved in the intelligence and policy relating to Iraq.

MB: Our focus was then on dealing with the manifestations of terrorist threats in the United Kingdom since 9/11. Our work was increasing exponentially. It increased very much more when we went into Iraq, but our main focus was dealing with the protection of the United Kingdom.

PRASHAR: But how complete was the intelligence picture and how did your Service go about filling the gaps in relation to Iraq?

MB: The picture was not complete. The picture on intelligence never is. We regarded the threat, the direct threat, from Iraq as low but we did not believe he [Saddam Hussein] had the capability to do anything much in the UK. That turned out to be the right judgment.

FREEDMAN: Can I just ask one question, which is related to the things that Iraqis might have done – the proposition that Saddam's regime were providing support to al-Qaida and even might have been involved in 9/11. Did you give any credence to these sorts of assessment?

MB: No. It was not a judgment that found favour with some parts of the American machine. To my mind Iraq, Saddam Hussein had nothing to do with 9/11 and I have never seen anything to make me change my mind.

LYNE: The Foreign Affairs Committee of the House of Commons in 2004 concluded that war in Iraq had possibly made terrorist attacks against British nationals and British interests more likely in the short-term. Now, how significant in your view a factor was Iraq compared with other situations that were used by extremists, terrorists, to justify their actions?

MB: I think it is highly significant and the JIC [Joint Intelligence Committee] assessments that I have reminded myself of say that. By 2003/2004 we were receiving an increasing number of leads to terrorist activity from within the UK and the – our involvement in Iraq radicalised, for want of a better word, a whole generation of young people, some British citizens, not a whole generation, a few among a generation, saw our involvement in Iraq as being an attack on Islam. So although the media has suggested that in July 2005, the attacks on 7/7, that we were surprised these were British citizens, that is not the case because really there had been an increasing number of British-born

65

individuals living and brought up in this country, some of them third generation, who were attracted to the ideology of Osama bin Laden and saw the west's activities in Iraq and Afghanistan as threatening their fellow religionists and the Muslim world. So it undoubtedly increased the threat.

LYNE: Were there other attacks or planned attacks in which you had evidence that Iraq was a motivating factor?

MB: Yes. I mean, if you take the videos that were retrieved on various occasions after various plots, where terrorists who had expected to be dead explained why they had done what they did, it features. It is part of what we call the single narrative, which is the view of some that everything the west was doing was part of a fundamental hostility to Islam, which pre-dated 9/11, but it was enhanced by those events. Arguably we gave Osama bin Laden his Iraqi jihad so that he was able to move into Iraq in a way that he wasn't before.

LYNE: To what extent did the conflict in Iraq exacerbate the overall threat that your Service and your fellow services were having to deal with from international terrorism?

MB: Substantially. The fact is that the threat increased, was exacerbated by Iraq, and caused not only my Service but many other services round the world to have to have a major increase in resources to deal with it.

FREEDMAN: As part of the war, your view was that a war in Iraq would aggravate the threat from whatever source to the United Kingdom?

MB: Yes.

FREEDMAN: How did you communicate this view to the prime minister?

MB: Through the JIC [Joint Intelligence Committee] assessments which I fed in.

FREEDMAN: The issue was there?

MB: I can't tell you to what extent senior ministers read the JIC assessments. I don't know the answer to that. I believe they did read them. But if they read them, they can have had no doubt.

FREEDMAN: Thank you.

LYNE: You did not have a practice of regular, scheduled, bilateral, one-on-one meetings with Mr Blair?

MB: No.

LYNE: So if messages were to get through to the prime minister about the expected impact of the Iraq war on terrorism, it would have come through your participation in joint meetings, through the home secretary?

MB: Yes. I believe the head of SIS [MI6] saw him much more frequently than I did, for understandable reasons.

LYNE: Thank you.

MB: I think that the JIC has about it an aura which is undeserved. People talk in hushed tones about the Joint Intelligence Committee. It is another Whitehall committee. It is fallible. I think it was pretty good on the terrorist threat actually; much less good on Iraq.

Throughout my career, even when quite junior, I have been involved in helping ministers to understand the inadequacies of intelligence.

CHILCOT: Thank you.

NADIA: The day I saw the tanks leave the government was celebrating, but not the people. It was said we were free from the coloniser and masters of our country. For me those words were hollow. They reminded me of Saddam's speeches.

Baghdad is the city of ghosts. Death has become background music. Daily we are confronted with coffins and funeral tents while explosions turn our skies black. In Iraq families announce a death with black and white cloth. They write the name of their loved on and hang it from the walls of their house. The streets are covered with cloth. All you see is black and white.

The moment Saddam fell, my country was torn apart. Before you never heard of Sunni, Shia or Kurd but now sectarianism divides us and ISIS roam our land.

I was teaching at a Shia University when I got the letter. The second we finished the final exam I had to pack up my bags and go. The head of my department said she had received an envelope with a bullet and my name. Before I left, I stood in the garden where I first saw the bombs come down. It was spring. The Gardenia tree was beginning to bloom these small white flowers. It was fresh, almost new. You smell it and you want to be a child again. My family came to Baghdad – five sisters, three brothers, nine nieces – to say goodbye. We were all gathered under the tree and my niece Diyan grabbed my knees. Everyone always says she is like a younger me. She grabbed me hard, wouldn't let go and asked me to take her with me. But we were a big family. They couldn't come.

It was 4.30 and I was leaving the University. Lectures were over. There was only one gate out of school and all 4,000 students were leaving that way. I heard shouting, then an explosion at the gate. There was a suicidal guy. He just pulled the trigger. There was fire, parts of bodies scattered and the smell of powder. I saw my students start to run. Then we heard a second one. A car bomb. They were full of life and there they were, lying on the streets of Baghdad. These were our children. They are Iraq's lost generation.

Chilcot? No, I haven't heard of Chilcot.